METROPOLITAN
FLOWERS

THE
METROPOLITAN MUSEUM of ART,
NEW YORK
HARRY N. ABRAMS, INC.,
PUBLISHERS,
NEW YORK

METROPOLITAN FLOWERS

Text by
EVERETT FAHY
Design by
ALVIN GROSSMAN

Published by The Metropolitan Museum
of Art, New York
Bradford D. Kelleher, Publisher
John P. O'Neill, Editor in Chief
Margot Feely, Project Supervisor
Ellyn Allison, Editor
Alvin Grossman, Designer

Copyright ©1982 by The Metropolitan
Museum of Art

Library of Congress Cataloging in Publi-
cation Data

Metropolitan Museum of Art (New York,
N.Y.)
    Metropolitan flowers.

    1. Flowers in art.   2. Art—New
York (N.Y.)   3. Metropolitan Museum
of Art (New York, N.Y.)
I. Fahy, Everett.
II. Title
N7680.M47 1982   704.9'434   82-8091
ISBN 0-87099-310-0   AACR2
ISBN 0-8109-1317-8 (Abrams)

The photographs for this volume were
taken by Walter J.F. Yee, Sheldan Collins,
Lynton Gardiner, Gene C. Herbert, and
Alexander Mikhailovich, The Photograph
Studio, The Metropolitan Museum of Art,
with the exception of those on pages 52-
53, by Malcolm Varon.

Composition by Innovative Graphics
International, Ltd., New York
Printed and bound by Dai Nippon
Printing Co., Ltd., Tokyo, Japan

TITLE PAGE. Roses, peonies, tulips, German Irises, morning glories, and other
flowers of a late spring garden are com-
bined with fruits and a nest of eggs in this
painting by Severin Roesen (American,
died 1871) entitled *Still Life: Flowers and
Fruit*. Roesen began his career in Ger-
many as a painter of porcelains and
brought to his new homeland the tradi-
tions of the European Baroque. Certainly
not an innovative painter by comparison
with his contemporaries in France (pp.
102–3), Roesen nevertheless achieved a
richness and verisimilitude admired in his
own time, and in ours as well.

FRONT AND BACK ENDPAPERS. *Iris and
Bridge*. Details of a six-panel screen, by
Ogata Kōrin (Japanese, 1658–1716), Edo
period. See description, p. 31.

HALF TITLE. *Fall-front Secretary*. Detail;
part of a bedroom suite by Herter
Brothers (American, working 1865/66–
1905/6); 1882. See description, p. 95.

OPPOSITE. *The Creation, and the Expulsion of Adam and Eve from Paradise*.
Painting by Giovanni di Paolo (Italian,
Sienese, 1403?–1482/83). See Introduction, p. 7.

OVERLEAF. *Self-Portrait*. Painting by
Gerard Dou (Dutch, 1613–1675). See Introduction, p. 7.

Introduction

Metropolitan Flowers differs from other books about flowers in art in one important respect: all the illustrations are reproduced from objects in the collections of the Metropolitan Museum. With examples drawn from the art of ancient China to that of today, it reflects the range of the Museum's almost encyclopedic holdings. In textiles, ceramics, furniture, prints, drawings, and paintings, it shows how artists throughout the world have shared the pleasures we experience whenever we see plants come into bloom. With their wonderful variety of shapes, colors, and scents, flowers gratify our sense of beauty. Watching them reappear every year also reinforces our hopes for the future.

In Western civilizations flowers are associated with the idea of paradise. The notion of an original golden age in which men and women enjoy perpetual spring runs through Greco-Roman literature. For Muslims paradise is an enclosed garden, and for Jews and Christians it is the Garden of Eden. The Metropolitan possesses a delightful portrayal of the latter in a predella panel, *The Creation, and the Expulsion of Adam and Eve from Paradise* (preceding pages) by Giovanni di Paolo (Italian, 1403?–1482/83). While God the Father points to the barren world he has just created, the Archangel Gabriel pushes Adam from a glade of golden apple trees underplanted with carnations, lilies, and roses. The four openings below the garden represent the rivers that flow to the four corners of the earth. Explorers would soon discover flowering plants far more exotic than those the artist painted. With the Age of Discovery not only were unfamiliar plants introduced into the Old World from the New, but new flowers were literally created by crossbreeding. One of the pleasures of looking at the art of past centuries is to see how certain flowers vary from their modern hybrids.

In the Orient flowers have always been held in high esteem: the earliest surviving silk scrolls, the so-called bird-and-flower paintings of the Sung dynasty (960–1279), demonstrate not only that the Chinese could paint flowers with astonishing accuracy but also that they regarded flowers as a suitable subject for high art, long before Westerners took floral art seriously. As A. Hyatt Mayor once wrote:, "The Chinese and Japanese painters felt their way beyond the plum branch held in their hands into the swing and life of all blossoming trees."

Our distant ancestors' initial interest in flowering plants must have been utilitarian: from blossoms come fruit and seed to sustain human life. Since some plants also have medicinal qualities, they were soon invested with magical powers that became associated with religious beliefs. Hence the figures from ancient myths who were transformed into flowers: Ajax, the larkspur; Adonis, the anemone; Clytie, the sunflower; and Narcissus, Hyacinthus, and Crocus, to name but a few.

The ancient practice of making pictures of flowers in order to identify useful plants led in the Middle Ages to the compilation of illustrated herbals. Simultaneously, the blossoms of some plants acquired symbolic meaning; in religious paintings this was often eclipsed by the artists' delight in depicting them. Later, in the Renaissance, scientific interest in the natural world prompted artists like Dürer and Leonardo to create some of the most truthful—and most beautiful—drawings of flowers ever made.

In Europe during the seventeenth century the study of plants reached a high point, and the increased knowledge is reflected in the botanical accuracy of the art of the period. This can be seen in the *Self-Portrait* (facing page) of Gerard Dou (Dutch, 1613–1675). One of Rembrandt's students, he presents himself to us as a prosperous artist-gentleman, resting his arm on the stone casement of his studio. A carefully observed grapevine, laden with fruit, clambers up the wall on the right, while on the left an ornate urn holds a pot marigold or calendula. Provided the plant is kept in a warm and sunny place during the winter, it can bloom all year long. Thus the calendula is one of the few plants that defies the rules of nature. To enjoy the others on a year-round basis we must turn to the work of artists who have given lasting life to the ephemeral beauty of flowers.

The invitation to write this book came from John O'Neill and Margot Feely, who learned of my interest in flowers from John Pope-Hennessy. The project could not have been realized without their personal commitment and unstinting aid. I am particularly indebted to Mary Steel whose intelligence and perseverance aided me in more ways than I can describe, to Ellyn Allison for her skill with a blue pencil, and to members of the Museum's Editorial Department, Mary Laing and Kathleen Howard. The talents of Alvin Grossman must here be noted—he made the book take shape. To the curators of the Metropolitan Museum, many of them old friends from the days when I was a member of the Department of European Paintings, I owe thanks for their willing help and enthusiasm, and I am grateful to my colleagues at The Frick Collection for their patience while I was spending time on *Metropolitan Flowers*. The book owes much to the discerning eye of the late A. Hyatt Mayor, who during his long and distinguished career at the Metropolitan Museum was the author of many works including three calendars devoted to flowers and gardens. They have been freely used in making the selections that follow.

May I add a note of warning? I have done my best to identify flowers, but I am not a trained botanist, just a keen amateur gardener who loves pictures. I am bound to have made some mistakes for which I beg the reader's indulgence.

Everett Fahy

Throughout his long life Claude Monet (French, 1840–1926) celebrated the beauty of flowers. Not only did he paint them with evident pleasure but also he was an avid gardener, growing annuals near houses he rented at Argenteuil and Vétheuil, and ultimately building a large garden for herbaceous plants by the house he bought at Giverny.

The flowering plants seen in *Terrace at Sainte-Adresse* are the ones that light up the majority of European and American gardens in midsummer, and in this ambitious canvas of 1867 Monet plays off their brilliant colors to marvelous effect. The tall spikes of red gladioli, echoing the vertical lines of the flagpoles, repeat the color of the flags, as do the red and yellow blossoms of the nasturtiums sprawling along the ledge in the foreground and creeping up the fence on the right. Probably the red and white flowers in the central bed are geraniums and the three patches of blue in the bed on the right are ageratums. As gardens go it is conventional, not at all unlike the beds of familiar flowers that reappear every summer in front of French train stations.

This extraordinary embroidered rug was made between 1832 and 1835 by Zeruah Higley Guernsey, a young woman in Castleton, Vermont. She married Memri Caswell in 1846, and this embroidery is now known as the Caswell Carpet. Stitched into the carpet are the initials of Mrs. Caswell's maiden name and the initials of two Potawatomi Indians who were studying at Castleton Medical College. They were boarders in Zeruah's home and presumably helped embroider the carpet.

Most of the seventy-six panels display floral motifs; Zeruah Guernsey's garden may have inspired many of these designs, and she may also have used a pattern book. In the panel at the left a couple walks in a garden whose gigantic five-petaled flowers the Douanier Rousseau might have admired. There is no serpent in this Garden of Eden; rather the flowers and the fruit seem to signify the bounty of the New World. Here Adam and Eve are transformed into a prosperous New England couple whose union has blossomed and become fruitful.

Ancient Persian gardens were small, paved enclosures in which water played an important part. A typical garden, such as the one shown here, consisted of a small central pool and channels for water that divided the retreat into fourths, an allusion to the four corners of the globe. This illustration from an early sixteenth-century Bukharan copy of the thirteenth-century poem *Būstān* ("Garden of Perfume"), shows the king of Syria, seated on a dais, conversing with paupers. To judge from the plants in bloom, it is spring. Trees growing outside the walls of the garden have burst into bloom, and plants resembling primulas and hollyhocks grow in the L-shaped beds. Two blue Persian Irises flower in the lower left, while a third, a bronze-colored specimen, blossoms to the right of the sultan, against the gold ground.

Flowers in art are often associated with heightened states of being. In the seventeenth-century Persian plate shown above, a young woman holds a wine cup that is an allusion to the intoxication of love or perhaps of mysticism. The lush, freely drawn flowers create a paradisal environment.

Allegorical descriptions of the five senses are embroidered in a variety of stitches and materials on a seventeenth-century English box. On the lid, flowers grow to luxuriant size and beasts are charmed by the music of the lady with a lute, who represents the sense of hearing.

At least three distinct varieties of lilies bloom in the outer border surrounding this seventeenth-century miniature of the Mughal general Qulich Khan. The one with magenta-pink recurved petals is called the Turk's Cap Lily because its pendulous flowers reminded European gardeners of outlandish Muslim headgear. Also depicted are lilies with pink upward-facing blossoms and lilies with large upright orange trumpets, as well as a myriad of other flowers, including a clump of Persian Cyclamens in the upper right corner. Nothing is known about the artist responsible for these delightful flowers; his task was merely to decorate the page on which the portrait miniature by Lalchand was mounted so that it could be preserved in an album along with portraits of other grandees and columns of calligraphy.

Strictly speaking, the day lilies in the Chinese watercolor (overleaf) are not lilies at all. They belong to a different botanical genus, *Hemerocallis,* a name derived from the Greek meaning beautiful for a day. Though the flowers are short-lived, the plants bloom profusely, often providing a three- or four-week display. A native of China and Japan, the day lily was imported by Westerners but soon escaped from their gardens and naturalized itself as a wildflower throughout Europe and North America. In recent decades, commercial growers have changed the day lily so much that our modern hybrids would probably be unrecognizable to Ch'en Shun (1483–1544), the Ming-dynasty artist whose swift brush caught the vigorous quality of the arching grasslike leaves and the rigid stems with their exuberant orange blossoms.

This *Annunciation,* the central panel of a portable altarpiece, was painted as accurately as possible, and every domestic detail is exactly what one would expect to find in an early fifteenth-century Flemish dwelling. The painter was Robert Campin (active 1406–died 1444), who, with his somewhat younger contemporary Jan van Eyck, perfected the technique of oil painting. By mixing brilliant colors with fluid oil, these early Netherlandish artists were able to describe the subtlest gradations of light, so that individual objects in their paintings appear astoundingly realistic. It only remained for the Italians of the early Renaissance to master the science of linear perspective, creating illusions that are totally convincing.

To modern eyes the objects on the table may seem to be no more than a pleasing still life, but to Campin's contemporaries they had symbolic meaning. The candle sends up a wisp of smoke because the divine radiance of the Archangel Gabriel has snuffed out its flame. In many paintings of the Annunciation he holds a lily, an allusion to the Virgin's lily-white purity; here it is placed in a vase, as if a decoration for a table. Commonly known as a Madonna or Easter Lily, this deliciously fragrant flower has been cultivated in gardens for thousands of years. The Minoans depicted it in frescos and the Assyrians carved it in bas-reliefs. During the Greco-Roman era it was associated with the goddess of love, and only in Christian times did it become an emblem of chastity.

At first glance, the magnificent blossoms in this woodblock print may appear to be sheer fantasy. Each flower head looks different, some with long petals reaching out like antennae, some with short petals forming compact globes. This diversity is not the invention of the artist, Andō Hiroshige (Japanese, 1797–1858); it is his reportage, in a decorative vocabulary, of hundreds of years of crossbreeding and elaborate methods of cultivation. For centuries the Japanese have given this flower pride of place in their gardens, and in a very stylized form it appears as their national emblem, the rising sun. Until 1886, when many ancient customs were abolished, a chrysanthemum festival was held each year in November. Moving slowly along the paths of the imperial gardens, the Japanese emperor and his courtiers ceremoniously inspected and admired bed after bed of the richly colored blossoms.

In Europe the chrysanthemum has a much shorter history than in the Orient. Brought from China to Marseilles in 1789, it became established in French and English gardens following the Napoleonic Wars. European hybridists created a new type called the Pompon Chrysanthemum, a small-flowered variety with a loose, branching habit. Claude Monet (1840–1926) painted several bouquets of them in 1880–81. (Although his *Chrysanthemums* shown at the left bears the date 1882—the year he sold it—we know for certain that it was painted during the fall of 1880.) Thus, a decade before his famous series of haystacks, poplar trees, and the facade of Rouen Cathedral, the French artist had developed an interest in painting versions of the same subject.

Like the chrysanthemum itself, this late nineteenth-century Chinese ceremonial or "happy occasion" robe, shown in detail, is notable for the variety and richness of its colors. Designed for a woman of the opulent Manchu aristocracy, the robe's eight silk-embroidered roundels of ornamental chrysanthemums glisten against a vibrant background. Associated with many desirable and pleasant things—the rich season of autumn, long life, and joviality—the chrysanthemum appears as a decorative motif in a wide range of oriental objects, from textiles to weapons.

The traditional title of this masterpiece by Edgar Degas (French, 1834–1917), *A Woman with Chrysanthemums,* is somewhat misleading. Most of the bouquet consists of hardy asters, recognizable by their dense fringe of petals surrounding large golden centers. They range from white to mauve to blue—a color never seen in chrysanthemums. The vase also holds some orange and yellow daisy-like flowers that may be coreopsis. But this is not to say there are no chrysanthemums here. These plants usually come into bloom when asters are at their peak, so some of the freely painted blossoms may be chrysanthemums.

Just as the flowers look as though they had been thrust into the large bowl with no apparent design, so the picture itself has a casual quality that distinguishes it from the formal flowerpieces of the seventeenth and eighteenth centuries. The canvas is dated twice: Degas's first subject, in 1858, was the glorious mass of autumn blooms; the introspective woman was added seven years later.

The iris, which takes its name from the Greek personification of the rainbow, flourishes in temperate zones of the Northern Hemisphere. This woodblock print by Katsushika Hokusai (1760–1849) depicts the spectacular *Iris kaempferi*. When fully open, the petals extend horizontally. Tawny beige flowers, some edged in dark blue, are so compelling that one almost misses the grasshopper, which has already made a substantial dent in one of the spiky leaves. The colors of the irises are unusual but not impossible; the *kaempferi* is notable for the wide range of its hues and the abundance of its color combinations. Hokusai, who often signed his works with the characters that translate as "old man mad about painting," was extraordinarily prolific. He has always been among the Japanese artists best known and admired in the West. His treatment of nature and all of its elements shows not only accuracy and sensitivity but also a heightened response to beauty.

The cobalt-blue *Iris laevigata* with floppy petals forms the subject of this detail (left) of a pair of screens painted by Ogata Kōrin (1658–1716), one of the most famous Japanese decorative artists. The gray bridge to be seen in the fuller detail (front and back endpapers) was an amenity for visitors to the garden since this oriental iris must be grown in several inches of water.

The watercolor of two native American plants was painted in 1887 by John LaFarge (American, 1835–1910). The sturdy iris grows in coastal areas from Nova Scotia to Georgia. Its frequent companion the *rugosa* rose is a rambling shrub with an abundance of thorns. To some eyes these wildflowers with delicate hues and simple forms are as beautiful as any showy hybrid.

In May 1890, a few days before he left the asylum at Saint-Rémy in Provence, Vincent van Gogh (Dutch, 1853–1890) completed this still life of a pitcher filled with irises. Two months later he shot himself. Like most of his late paintings, this canvas shows a feverish intensity. What a contrast these tortured flowers make with the silky iris in the seventeenth-century flowerpiece by Nicolaes van Veerendael (p. 65).

Van Gogh's subject is the common flag or German Iris, remarkable for its fruity scent. It differs from the oriental irises on the preceding pages in the form of its petals: the three lowest ones have tufts of short hairs, hence the flower's other familiar name, the bearded iris. Yet another European variety, the Florentine Iris, was adopted by Louis VII of France as his emblem. It was first known as the fleur-de-Louis, but the name was later corrupted to fleur-de-lis.

The contrast between these two paintings of sunflowers underscores the difference between Claude Monet (1840–1926), the true impressionist who captures the radiant vitality of a superb bouquet, and Vincent van Gogh (1853–1890), the expressionist who makes an almost menacing image of two dried blossoms lying lifeless against a blue background. In a letter of December 1888, van Gogh wrote, "Gauguin was telling me the other day that he had seen a picture by Claude Monet of sunflowers in a large Japanese vase, very fine, but—he likes mine better. I don't agree." The picture Gauguin admired is probably the still life of 1887 shown below.

Sunflowers by Monet (dated 1881, but actually done in 1880) was probably painted indoors on a day when bad weather prevented the artist from working outside.

Sunflower seeds were brought to Europe from Peru and Mexico as early as the sixteenth century. Their botanical name (*Helianthus*) refers to the mistaken belief that the flower heads turn to follow the course of the sun.

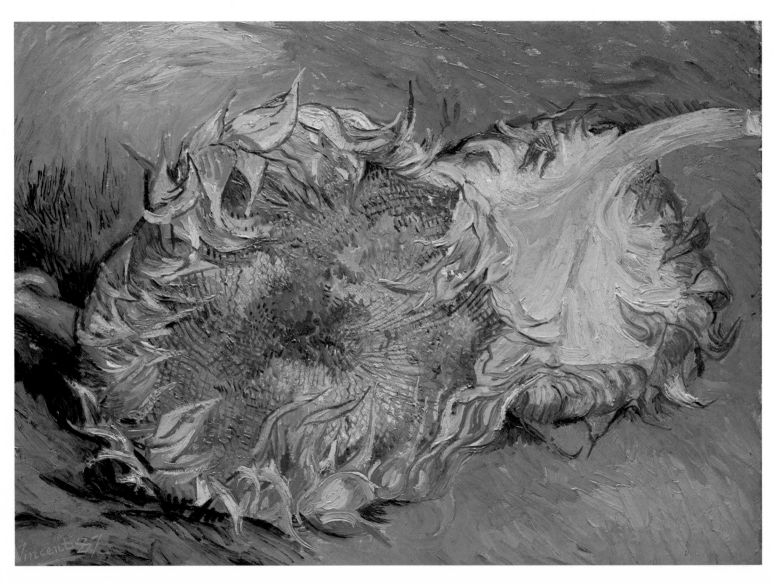

Hybrid Amaryllis Regina vittata.

The amaryllis is one of the most spectacular house plants. Its enormous funnel-shaped flowers are produced on rigid stems, often before the straplike foliage appears. Lucky growers may have a bulb that will send up more than one stem, as can be seen in the two-part monotype, dated 1977, by the American artist Mary Frank (born 1933). The colored engraving at far left by William Say (British, 1768–1834), based on a drawing by a certain Miss B. Cotton, was published in 1824. It documents a hybrid, started from a seed four years earlier, of an African variety that is distinguished by a greenish white star in the throat.

Derived from the Greek word meaning to shine, Amaryllis is the name of a shepherdess in Virgil's *Bucolics*. The correct botanical name of the flower, however, is *Hippeastrum*, from the Greek for horseman and star. The naming of plants is often delightfully capricious, and nomenclature continues to change, thanks to the research of botanists.

In the fourteenth century, Nō, originally a symbolic mimetic dance, was developed into full-fledged drama. This late seventeenth- or early eighteenth-century robe of silk and metal thread is the Nō costume called a *kara-ori*. The term not only defines the kind of wear—the outer garment used for female roles—but is the word that translates as "Chinese weaving," describing the embroidery-like texture of the fabric. The design is a simple variety of tree peony, albeit fantastically hued, seen through a golden lattice. The tree peony was grown in Japan as early as the eighth century, and ever since that time it has been regarded as a flower of singular beauty.

In its original form the tree-peony blossom was single, a simple aureole of petals around a golden center, but the varieties developed in the Chinese imperial garden are lavishly petaled. The first cultivated specimens grew in the gardens of the T'ang dynasty more than a thousand years ago, and some were so highly regarded they were given splendid names: King of Flowers and Hundred Ounces of Gold.

Today the tree peony flourishes in more than three hundred varieties. For the Chinese it is a symbol of spring and an emblem of love and affection. They regard it as the flower both of masculinity (the *yang* principle) and of feminine beauty.

Life-size tree peonies are the subject of the hanging silk scroll by Yun Shou-p'ing (1633–1690). With a lovely sense of decorative placement, he gives us a truthful record of enormous silken blossoms with ruffled and fringed petals. As would not occur in nature, however, flowers of different hues appear on the same bush. Perhaps the artist here has also given us an example of the art of grafting–a technique not unknown to Chinese gardeners of the time.

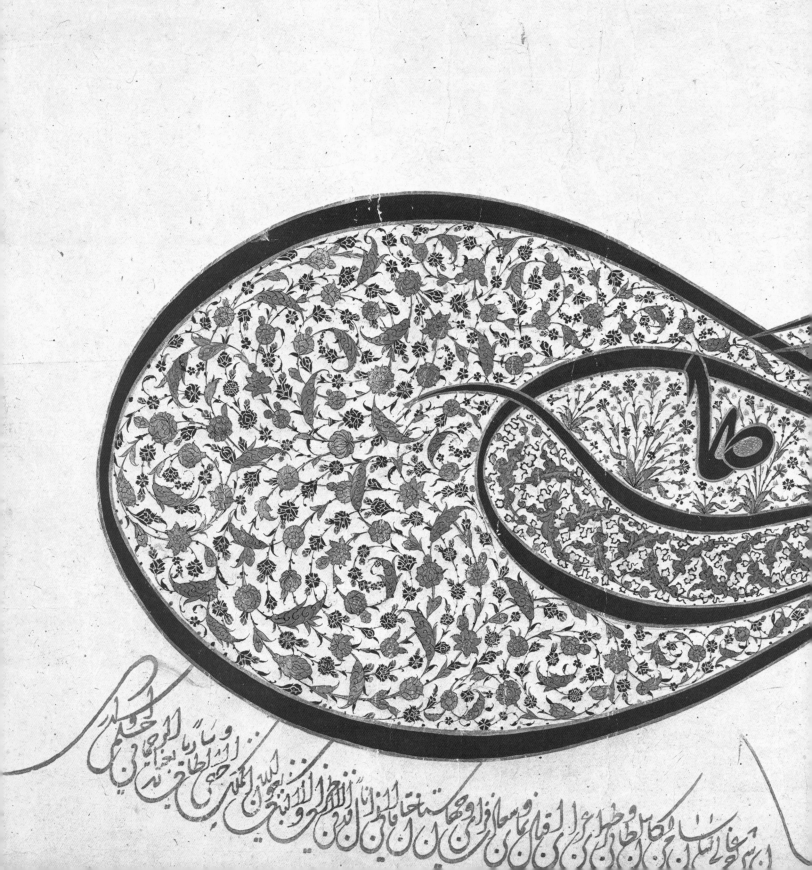

Moreljon.

From the earliest times calligraphy was practiced throughout Islam, and this art of beautiful writing was, in fact, more esteemed than that of painting. Within the Ottoman Empire the sultan's official signature was a tughra, or calligraphic emblem, executed by an official skilled in this art. The tughra, with its magnificent movement of line and delicacy of floral decoration, is one of the most typical and original creations of Ottoman art, and there is nothing comparable to it in other parts of the Muslim world.

One of the most elaborate and monumental of these devices—that of Sulaymān the Magnificent, who reigned from 1520 to 1566—appears on the preceding pages. A detail of this tughra at far left shows a stand of carnations, a flower for which the Ottoman Turks had a special fondness.

Their profusion and fragrance may have been emblematic of the bounty and virtue of Sulaymān. The stylization of these blossoms contrasts with the careful realism of the carnation depicted in a seventeenth-century Netherlandish watercolor at the left. It was mounted in a book containing more than fifty varieties of carnations. Ironically, this particular hybrid named Moreljon, whose ancestors were brought from the Near East by the Crusaders, has become rather more exotic than its eastern relatives. The charming field flower used by the Muslims to flavor drinks and sherbets has become an elegant botanical specimen.

In fifteenth-century Europe the carnation, or pink, signified faithful love and became an emblem of betrothal and marriage. In Italian portraits either the man or the woman may hold the flower, whereas in Northern European paintings it is more usually held by the bride. A delightful late fifteenth-century Flemish example is *Lady with a Pink* (left) attributed to Hans Memling (active about 1465–died 1494). This pert young woman is richly and fashionably dressed. The crimson of the flower is repeated in the deeper crimson of her gown. Like the fresh pink, she is in the springtime of her life. But although the flower is a symbol of undying love, its life is measured in days. The darker theme —the transience of human life and happiness—often underlies floral imagery. Thus, in *Lady with a Pink* (right) by Rembrandt (Dutch, 1606–1669), an older woman seems lost in poignant memories. Her springtime has passed, but she remains faithful to the love she once pledged. The woman, who may have been Rembrandt's daughter-in-law, is also portrayed in *The Jewish Bride*, one of his late masterpieces in the Rijksmuseum.

Sweetbriar and jasmine are the offering of a bright-haired angel in this painting by Cosimo Rosselli (Italian, Florentine, 1439–1507) entitled *Madonna and Child with Angels.* Sweetbriar, a five-petaled rose with a yellow center, grows wild throughout Europe. Jasmine, a deliciously perfumed flower with trumpet-like blossoms, is a symbol of Divine Love in Renaissance paintings, and to this day Italian brides include sprigs of it in their wedding bouquets. Glimpses of the Tuscan countryside can be seen at either side of the tabernacle, with the dome of the cathedral of Florence visible at the right.

Neither François Boucher (French, 1703–1770) nor Jean Honoré Fragonard (French, 1732–1806) chose to paint flowers with the botanical accuracy that some of their French contemporaries achieved, yet blossoms pervade their lighthearted compositions. For both artists flowers speak of love. In *The Toilet of Venus,* a canvas Boucher painted in 1751 for the room that housed Mme de Pompadour's bath, pink and blue roses lie in drifts across the step at the goddess's foot. Like the smoking incense burner, they suggest the voluptuous aroma of her perfumed bath. In *The Love Letter,* an oil of the 1770s, Fragonard surprises a young woman and her watchful lapdog as she inhales the fragrance of a tightly wrapped bouquet. The note she holds is addressed to her suitor.

The Hunt of the Unicorn is a tale of chase and capture in a flowery setting. According to medieval legend, the mythical unicorn could not be caught except by a virgin maid in a garden enclosure, symbol of her chastity. This fragment is part of the fifth tapestry in the celebrated series of seven on the unicorn theme at The Cloisters.

Beneath a holly tree laden with berries, a horn-blowing huntsman signals the capture of the beast within a wattle fence threaded with white and red roses. The profusion of plants and trees has inspired another name for these woven pictures: *millefleurs*. In these "tapestries of a thousand flowers," sixteenth-century Franco-Flemish artisans interlaced silk, wool, and silver-gilt threads so intricately that botanists have been able to identify more than eighty-five different kinds of plants. In this tapestry, for example, we recognize the thorny *alba* and the *gallica*, or French Rose.

Toward the end of his life the great Flemish artist Peter Paul Rubens (1577–1640) painted himself, his second wife, and their son Peter Paul engaged in a delightful garden promenade. A comparison can be drawn between the enchanting tones of Hélène's petal-like complexion and the flush of roses against the column behind her in this picture entitled *Rubens and His Wife, Hélène Fourment, with Their Child.* These flowers are a variety of *Rosa centifolia,* "rose of a hundred petals." Grown first in late sixteenth-century Holland, this heavily scented flower was immortalized in the seventeenth century by Dutch and Flemish painters of realistic flowerpieces. The *centifolia* was so popular that Dutch gardeners developed more than two thousand varieties.

Some Chinese will not grow a thorny rose bush because they believe it might introduce a thorn of dissension into their domestic affairs. This has not prevented Chinese gardeners from producing untold varieties of roses. The introduction of Chinese roses into Europe at the end of the eighteenth century was a great horticultural event. Unlike native European roses, some oriental kinds flower repeatedly. By crossing European and Chinese varieties, gardeners created the modern tea rose, which blooms continuously from early summer until late autumn. In this detail of a Chinese handscroll of the Ch'ing dynasty (1644–1911), wandering branches are laden with blossoms. The unidentified painter applied his colors to silk with graceful precision. In a part of the scroll not shown, wasps throng about their nest built on a projecting branch. Here we see three of those insects, again notable for the detail with which they are painted, hovering about the heady pink blossoms. It seems a pity that this splendid rose, with its large protective thorns, should have been excluded from any garden.

The scarlet flowers dotting the sunny meadow in *Path in the Ile Saint-Martin, Vétheuil* are the common Red Poppies or Corn Poppies that brighten the fields of Europe and Britain in late spring. When Claude Monet (1840–1926) painted the view in 1880, this wildflower had no special significance, but ever since World War I it has commemorated the soldiers who fell in Flanders, where "poppies blow/ Between the crosses, row on row."

The opium poppy is the principal subject of the sinister painting by Otto Marseus van Schrieck (Dutch, 1619–1678), *Still Life with Poppy, Insects, and Reptiles*. The ancients associated the flower with Hypnos and Morpheus, the gods of sleep and dreams, because the plant's sap has sedative powers. Van Schrieck depicts the showy poppy from behind, perhaps because the face, with its thick fringe of petals, is more difficult to paint.

An inspired composition of clusters of poppies on a field of gold is probably by the Japanese artist Kitagawa Sosetsu. Painted about the middle of the seventeenth century, this hanging scroll shows several unusual varieties of Japanese Poppies. Many of the flowers have four petals—some pure white, some white edged with red, some white with red centers, and others pure red. The cultivation of poppies dates back to remote antiquity, but, in Europe, it was not until the advent of the Symbolists, the Decadents, and Art Nouveau toward the end of the nineteenth century and the beginning of the twentieth that poppies became a truly major design element in works of art.

The famous series of water lilies by Claude Monet (1840–1926) date from the last thirty years of his life. Soon after purchasing a house and property at Giverny, he laid out extensive flower beds and diverted a small stream to create a water garden. *Bridge over a Pool of Water Lilies,* of 1899, depicts the Japanese footbridge that forms an arching motif in many of his views of the garden. Unlike his later canvases, which have a flat, decorative quality, this picture makes a strong spatial illusion. The still surface of the water recedes deep into the picture, and clumps of floating lilies alternate with the shimmering reflections of overhanging plants.

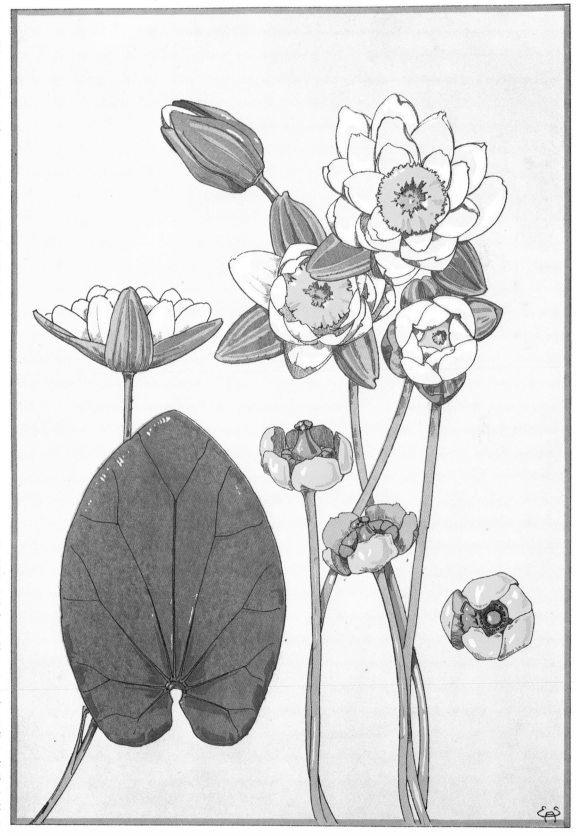

Water lilies belong to the genus *Nymphaea,* aquatic plants with floating leaves and cup-shaped flowers in shades of white, pink, yellow, and blue. There are two main types, a hardy variety whose flowers float on the surface, and a tropical variety that sends out much larger, more colorful flowers on long stems, perhaps a foot above the water. Both Monet and an early twentieth-century French artist, E. A. Séguy, have portrayed the first variety: the latter in the colored lithograph at the right, one of a series of his botanical prints that recalls the Japanese influence on Western art in the first decades of the twentieth century.

Beter man

Joncker.

Introduced into Europe from Constantinople in 1551, the tulip gained such popularity in Holland that between the years 1633 and 1637 wild speculation in bulbs known as tulipomania precipitated an economic disaster. Jacob Marrel (Dutch, 1614–1681) rendered the national flower in a watercolor dated 1636, describing with precision and delicacy the streaked blossom, or "broken" tulip. Though it is commonly known as the Rembrandt Tulip, the name is hardly accurate. Rembrandt is not known to have painted them.

This variety of tulip reappears along with *centifolia* roses, the bearded iris, hibiscus, jasmine, and other blooms in *Bouquet of Flowers in a Crystal Vase*, of 1662, by Nicolaes van Veerendael (Flemish, 1640–1691). A specialist in this sort of still life, Veerendael painted his subject with careful attention to detail but, typically, with a disregard for the seasons in which flowers grow. The dewdrops comment on the short-lived beauty of such flower arrangements and the transience of life.

Martin Johnson Heade (American, 1817–1904) painted many versions of the hummingbirds and exotic flowers that he encountered on trips to South America in the 1860s and 1870s. In *Hummingbird and Passionflowers,* the tiny bird perches upon the stalk of the spectacular tropical passionflower vine—so named because of the imagined resemblance of parts of the flower to the instruments of the Passion of Christ.

Orchids, a painting of extraordinary beauty by the Chinese artist Ma Lin (active about 1250), exemplifies the inclination of Southern Sung art toward lyricism and subjectivity. Here, in ink and delicate colors brushed on silk, a simple, asymmetrical composition mirrors the perfection toward which the skilled gardener strove. Difficult to grow, the *cymbidium* orchid was admired for its grace, delicacy, and fragrance. These small flowers are the ancestors of the modern hybrids that bear the same name.

To the eighteenth-century German settlers of the fertile farms of southeastern Pennsylvania, the vicinity where Johan Henrich Otto is known to have worked, the imaginative flowers of *Fraktur Motifs,* a decorative page he painted about 1790, would have been familiar, perhaps even identifiable. Like the farmers of the area, the artists and craftsmen were faithful to the old country in religion, language, and folk customs, preserving traditional elements of design on household items of every sort, from dower chests to iron stoves. Not the least among the treasured items were the documents that celebrated the happy events of family life—the marriage, birth, and baptismal certificates known as frakturs (a script that derived from a sixteenth-century German printing typeface). Executed in watercolor, these gaily decorated works often incorporated such flowers as the ever-popular tulip, sawtoothed carnation, and flamboyant fuchsia, continuing an ancient ornamental tradition ultimately rooted in Persian textiles (p. 72). This fine example is unusual because it is entirely ornamental. The heraldic arrangement of exuberant birds, crowns, and flowers may have been done purely for the artist's amusement.

69

The wallpaper shown here in a detail was the last to be designed by William Morris (1834–1896), the leading figure in the decorative arts of Victorian England. It dates from the year of his death and was named Compton, after the client's house for which it was intended. An exuberant yet perfectly controlled pattern dominated by poppies, tulips, and honeysuckle, with speedwells and pimpernels in a minor key, Compton is perhaps Morris's finest wallpaper, exemplifying his own dictum that "ornamental pattern work…

must possess three qualities: beauty, imagination, and order."

Morris was a socialist pioneer whose writings and work as a designer helped to revolutionize contemporary taste. No such ambition lies behind the piece of early nineteenth-century French embroidery shown above. Created as a salesman's sample, and exquisitely worked in satin stitch in pale silks on a dark velvet ground, this stylized poppy is the principal element of a border designed to bloom on some fortunate dandy's waistcoat.

Like the prayer rugs on which faithful Muslims kneel, this remarkable nineteenth-century embroidered hanging, made for a prayer niche, has as its central design the essential mihrab, or prayer niche, to indicate the direction of Mecca. Within the center springs the Tree of Life, a motif found in Iran as early as the seventh century and which spread to other countries through the export of embroideries. From the arabesque-patterned branches of this tree, and in its surrounding borders, a profusion of conventionalized flowers bloom: carnations and roses in medallion form, pomegranate blossoms, and clematis, to name but a few. The whole is made up of many small pieces of woolen cloth set into separate ground colors of olive-brown, white, red, and blue, all outlined and connected to form patterns by chain stitch in silk thread.

The decoration of this splendid baluster-shape vase is characteristic of the reign of the Chinese emperor K'ang Hsi (1662–1722). The style is known as *famille verte,* named for the apple green predominant in the palette of enamel colors that shimmer on the vase. The flowering branches springing from rocks could be those of any fruit tree of the genus *Prunus,* but since the leaves are few, it may well be a plum tree that is depicted here. Symbol of longevity, the plum sends out a profusion of blossoms on leafless and apparently dead branches. Perched among the five-petaled flowers are birds, perhaps wagtails.

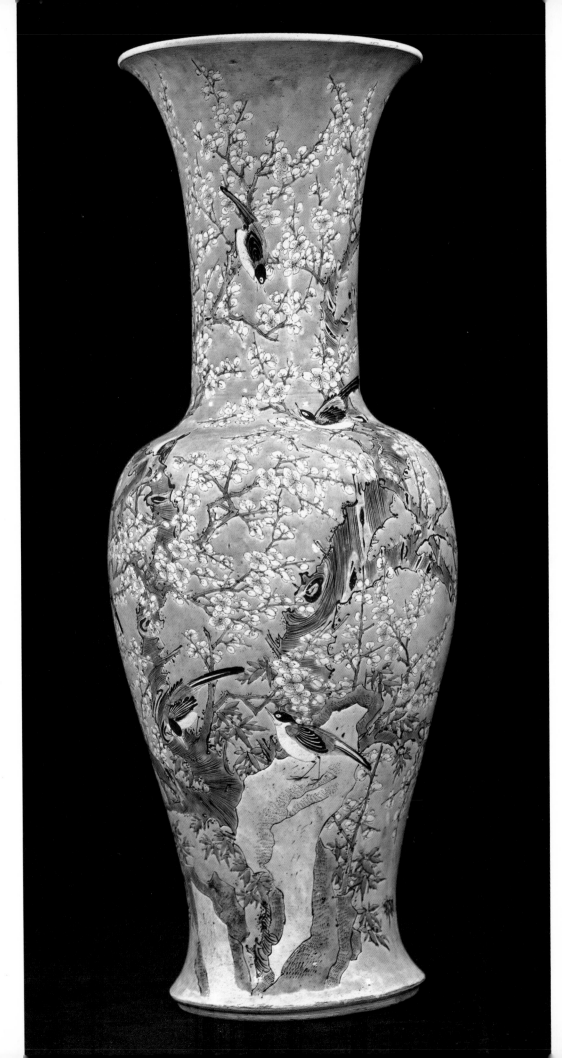

Plum blossoms in darkness were a favorite subject of the Japanese artist Suzuki Harunobu (1725–1770). Like a *haiku* poet, he enjoyed unexpected but delightful juxtapositions. In his woodblock print (right) a young woman casts the light of a lantern upward, and out of the darkness springs a dazzling spray of flowers.

Nature is precious in Japan, as is the beauty of women. Delicacy and refinement in the illustration of both is called for. The lid of the seventeenth-century leather box at far right has been lacquered in black, and the spray of plum blossoms inlaid with mother-of-pearl.

During the reign of Jahangir (1605–1628) the art of book illustration flourished in India. The Mughal emperor was a munificent patron and he maintained rigid standards of quality. The miniature shown at the left is from an album that was once part of the royal library. Jahangir was also an enthusiastic gardener, and it was his horticultural interests, perhaps, that directed the artist to render the blossoms of this flowering tree, seemingly a quince, with delicate detail.

In China, red is the color associated with the joyous occasion of marriage. Worn by the bride, it is also the color of the processional umbrella, the color of the thread that binds in union the couple's cups of wine and honey, and, appropriately, the background color of the early eighteenth-century embroidered wedding hanging shown in detail at the right. The stylized five-petaled blossoms flowering from golden branches can be identified as apricot, a variety of *Prunus,* the symbol of the fair sex.

In a glorious sweep of sensuous line, the renowned artist Kitagawa Utamaro (1753–1806) captures the Japanese devotion to the art of flower arrangement. This woodblock print of about 1795 is from a series illustrating a popular drama of the time. It describes a scene in which sake is offered in celebration of the moon festival to the man and woman who place flowers in a bamboo vase. In the inset the drama is further played out: a basket of cherry blossoms is brought to Lady Kawoyo to console her for the loss of her husband.

David Hockney (British, born 1937) visited Japan in November 1971, and shortly after he returned to London he painted this picture of stunning visual impact, *Mount Fuji and Flowers.* White flowers in a bamboo vase, set against a backdrop of the famous volcano, are a distillation of Japan to the Western eye.

These two pictures are early and late examples of the flowerpiece tradition. *A Vase with Flowers*, at right, was painted by Jacob Vosmaer (Dutch, 1584–1641) in 1615. It is a laboriously painted composition of roses, tulips, and irises, crammed into a brass pitcher and set on a ledge with a lizard. *Bouquet of Flowers* was executed about three hundred years later by Odilon Redon (French, 1840–

1916), the Symbolist who championed the idea that artists should not limit themselves to what they see. "True art," he wrote, "lies in a reality that is felt." This glowing arrangement of lilacs, anemones, tulips, and bachelor's buttons, mingled with flowers of Redon's imagination, captures all the atmosphere and fragrance of a freshly gathered spring bouquet.

The Sèvres plaque at the left is one of a pair set into the fall front of a secretary made by Martin Carlin between 1775 and 1780. The oval plaques were painted in 1773 by Mlle Xhrouet (French, active 1772–1778). In a wicker basket full-blown blossoms of peonies, poppies, a tulip, and morning glories are set off by a striped ribbon. Characteristic of Xhrouet's compositions are the massing of the largest, most intensely colored flowers on the right, and her evident delight in showing some of them from underneath and in profile.

In *Vase of Flowers*, exhibited at the Salon of 1781, a heavy bouquet of fanciful blossoms almost overwhelms a blue porcelain jar with gilt-bronze mounts. The small oval painting is signed and dated at lower right: "Mlle Vallayer/1780." The following year the artist, who had been admitted to the Académie Royale in 1770, married a lawyer and added his name to hers. Anne Vallayer-Coster (French, 1744–1818) is now widely regarded as one of the outstanding still-life painters of eighteenth-century France.

A charming informality distinguishes these early twentieth-century still lifes. Both depict tiny bouquets resting on tables that form part of larger, almost abstract compositions. In *Pansies on a Table*, an oil of about 1918 by Henri Matisse (French, 1869–1954), several pansies and a single carnation hold their own against the bold pattern of the background. Ten years later Sir William Nicholson (British, 1872–

1949) painted *Mauve Primulas on a Table*. The primulas stand in a glass with dimorphothecas, a South African flower with a dark center that had only recently been introduced into English gardens. Nicholson may have come to know these novel plants through Gertrude Jekyll, the landscape designer whose battered garden boots he immortalized in a canvas now in the Tate Gallery.

The French artist Henri Fantin-Latour (1836–1904) specialized in studies of flowers and fruits. *Still Life with Pansies* was painted in 1874, about the time he became interested in the music of Richard Wagner and began to paint some extraordinary figure groups.

Greek mythology tells us that pansies sprang up at the command of Zeus to supply forage for Io, whom the king of the gods had transformed into a heifer to protect her from his jealous spouse. In the lore of Christianity the flowers symbolize the Holy Trinity. In this painting pansies are shown in rustic containers—two terra-cotta pots and a market basket—and the informal presentation enhances the shy beauty of the flowers. Their vari-colored petals have a sheen, a velvety iridescence that almost makes us believe we are looking at real flowers instead of painted images.

The association of fruit and flowers in still life has a long tradition, and conscious echoes of it can be detected in these paintings by the French contemporaries Paul Cézanne (1839–1906) and Henri Fantin-Latour (1836–1904). By chance, even the placement of the flowers in the right background is the same in both works. But the artists' intentions were very different. Fantin-Latour's *Still Life with Flowers and Fruit*, on the right, signed and dated 1866, is a naturalistic rendering, in which the fragrant lilacs and white stocks, the wicker basket and the glossy fruit conjure up the realistic world of the senses. Some twenty to thirty years later Cézanne painted *Still Life: Apples and a Pot of Primroses*—a study of a pot of primulas and fruit strewn across a crumpled white cloth—to make a comment on the forms of things transposed from three-dimensional reality to the ambiguity of the picture plane. The painting once belonged to Monet.

Lavishly carved on the outside and brightly painted within, this late sixteenth-century French armoire was no doubt created as a marriage cabinet. Its decorative scheme, eluding tidy analysis, includes classical, biblical, and allegorical figures. In the painting shown here the sense of smell is personified by a young woman who with one hand holds a Madonna Lily to her nose and with the other balances a large urn of flowers precariously on her knees. The artist copied her and the elegant greyhound at her side from an engraving of *Odoratus* after Marten de Vos (1532–1603), adding for good measure the tortoise as footstool and the monkey eating an apple from other prints after de Vos representing the senses of touch and taste, respectively.

Part of a bedroom suite made by Herter Brothers of New York in 1882, this fall-front secretary epitomizes the so-called Eastlake style in the severe lines of its construction and the rich surface decoration of the inlay, which is based on natural forms. In the middle of the main panel a bulbous urn holds branches of stylized roses that spread symmetrically to fill the available space. Similar branches are arranged in a horizontal pattern on the drawers, springing from a central motif.

Sons of a German cabinetmaker, the half-brothers Gustav and Christian Herter were in partnership in New York City by 1866. Christian (1840–1883) later bought Gustav out and assumed control of the firm, which became one of the greatest decorating establishments in America. This secretary was made for the railroad tycoon Jay Gould, to whom it was invoiced on March 1, 1882: "1 Inlaid Ebony writing desk to match Bedroom Suite $550."

Personifying Spring, the late seventeenth-century Flora who looks out at left from the task of arranging flowers in an urn is Françoise-Marie de Bourbon, Mlle de Blois, legitimized daughter of Louis XIV and Mme de Montespan. The large embroidered hanging is one of an original set of eight depicting the Sun King, Mme de Montespan, and their children as the Elements and Seasons. Below Flora's feet, watering cans, a rake, a scythe, and other implements are a reminder that garden flowers must be cultivated before they can be enjoyed.

The small embroidered picture shown above presents the goddess of spring in quite a different guise. Seated stiffly in one corner, and clutching her emblematic flowers, she has been re-created in mid-eighteenth-century America by the imagination of a child. A pair of flop-eared rabbits disport themselves in honor of the season; one—perhaps a favorite pet—rests confidingly against Flora's skirts. On the back of the mounting is written: "Worked by Mary Wright at a school in Newport, R. I. 1754."

The art of appliquéd quiltmaking in America reached its height in the city of Baltimore in the years between 1846 and 1852 with a group of coverlets of a kind variously referred to as album, friendship, bride, freedom, or presentation quilts. They were composed of individually crafted blocks, each usually signed by the maker. This example of about 1845–50, though unsigned, appears to have been the work of one highly skilled person traditionally identified as Mary Evans.

This seems evident from the workmanship demanded to create the detailed latticework baskets and from the use of a white rose—her "signature"—tellingly placed to attract attention. There is an abundance of flowers in this Baltimore quilt—in baskets of various shapes, in urns, vases, wreaths, and bouquets—and all are shaped from carefully selected fabrics. The baskets of flowers, in composition and shading, bear close resemblance to the contemporary theorem paintings (see pp. 104–5).

Still Life: A Basket of Flowers was painted by the Flemish artist Jan Brueghel the Younger (1601–1678). It shows a collection of familiar flowers in a wicker basket. They have recently been gathered from garden and field and await the hand of a flower arranger. This colorful medley of blooms shows the attention to detail that is part of the tradition of flower painting established by artists of Brueghel's father's generation.

Wicker baskets are seldom seen in Baroque still-life paintings, for during this period artists preferred the rich colors and textures of glass and metal containers. They became popular in the late eighteenth and nineteenth centuries, when naturalism was prized and common things became fashionable (see pp. 84, 88–89, 91).

Eugène Delacroix (1798–1863), the most important painter of the Romantic movement in France, produced the beautiful *Basket of Flowers* in the tranquility of the country-side while Paris was suffering the political and social up-heavals caused by the Revolution of 1848. This large canvas is one of a series of five flower paintings by Delacroix, two of which—including this one—he showed in the Salon of 1849.

Dahlias, zinnias, and other late-summer flowers tumble out of an overturned wicker basket. The lushness of nature is emphasized by the white morning glories arching over the basket, which overflows like a cornucopia. An impression of movement is conveyed by the random play of vivid colors and by the flickering highlights on the foliage.

It is likely that *Yellow Basket of Flowers* was painted about 1825–50 by a cultivated young lady who attended one of the seminaries for females where, in nineteenth-century America, the curriculum included watercolor painting. The rules for the study of still life, as in all manner of things, were strict and, if meticulously followed, allowed even the less-than-talented student to achieve instant success. This young artist painted her picture on paper from a carefully applied stencil or "theorem," using paints she might have ground and mixed herself, achieving a result that would have pleased the most exacting instructor. A basket of nodding flowers is well represented in a nicely balanced composition that may have had its origins in albums of prints or in chintzes.

Landscape, Fruit and Flowers, a colored lithograph published in 1862 by Currier & Ives, reflects the tradition of the formal flowerpiece that began in the seventeenth century. Inspired by a Yankee muse, it was mass-produced for the parlors of nineteenth-century Americans. Recognizable in the background is a glimpse of the Hudson River Valley, not the Rhine, and at the left the hummingbird is attracted to a trumpet vine, a climbing plant native to North America.

LAND

.PE, FRUIT AND FLOWERS.

List of Illustrations

FRONT ENDPAPER. *Iris and Bridge*, detail
Ogata Kōrin (Japanese, 1658–1716); Edo period
Six-panel screen; ink, colors and gold leaf on paper; 70½ x 146¼ in.
Purchase, Louisa Eldridge McBurney Gift, 1953, 53.7.2

HALF TITLE. *Fall-front Secretary*, detail
See pp. 94–95

TITLE. *Still Life: Flowers and Fruit*, detail
Severin Roesen (American, died 1871)
Oil on canvas; 40 x 50⅜ in.
Charles Allen Munn Bequest, Fosburgh Fund, Inc. and
  Mr. and Mrs. William Middendorf II Gifts, and Henry G. Keasbey
  Bequest, 1967, 67.111

PAGES 4–5. *The Creation, and the Expulsion of Adam and Eve from Paradise*
Giovanni di Paolo (Italian, Sienese, 1403?–1482/83)
Tempera and gold on wood; 17¹⁵⁄₁₆ x 20½ in.
Robert Lehman Collection, 1975, 1975.1.31

PAGE 6. *Self-Portrait*
Gerard Dou (Dutch, 1613–1675)
Oil on wood; 19¾ x 15⅜ in.
Bequest of Benjamin Altman, 1913, 14.40.607

PAGES 8–9. *Terrace at Sainte-Adresse*
Claude Monet (French, 1840–1926); 1867
Oil on canvas; 38⅝ x 51⅛ in.
Purchased with special contributions and purchase funds given or
  bequeathed by friends of the Museum, 1967, 67.241

PAGES 10–11. *Caswell Carpet*, whole and detail
Zeruah Higley Guernsey Caswell (American, 19th century); 1832–35
Twill-weave woolen fabric embroidered in colored woolen yarns;
  160 x 147 in.
Gift of Katharine Keyes, in memory of her father, Homer Eaton
  Keyes, 1938, 38.157

PAGES 12–13. *Salih, the Ayyubid King of Syria, Conversing with Two
  Paupers*, whole and detail
Leaf from a Būstān of Sa'di, folio 80 verso
Artist unknown (Central Asian, mid-16th century); Bukhara
Ink, colors, and gold on paper; 11½ x 7¾ in.
Frederick C. Hewitt Fund, 1911, 11.134.2

PAGE 14. *Plate*
Artist unknown (Northwest Iranian, 17th century)
"Kubatchi," composite body, painted and glazed; diam. 13⅞ in.
Mr. and Mrs. Isaac D. Fletcher Collection, Bequest of Isaac D.
  Fletcher, 1917, 17.120.56

PAGE 15. *The Five Senses: Hearing*, detail
Artist unknown (English, mid-17th century)
Box; wood, silk, metal thread, linen, pearls, mica; 5¾ x 9 x 7½ in.
Rogers Fund, 1929, 29.23.1

PAGES 16–17. *Portrait of Qulich Khan*, whole and detail
Lalchand (Indian, second quarter 17th century) and unknown artist;
  Mughal period
Leaf from an album; ink, colors, and gold on paper; 15¼ x 10⁵⁄₁₆ in.
Funds given by the Kevorkian Foundation supplementing the Rogers
  Fund, 1955, 55.121.10.30

PAGES 18–19. *Day Lilies*, detail
Ch'en Shun (Chinese, 1483–1544); Ming dynasty
Ink and colors on paper; 12¾ x 22¾ in.
Lent by Douglas Dillon, L.1981.15.16

PAGES 20–21. *Annunciation*, center panel of the Campin Altarpiece,
  whole and detail
Robert Campin (Flemish, active 1406– died 1444)
Oil on wood; 25¼ x 24⅞ in.
The Cloisters Collection

PAGES 22–23. *Chrysanthemums*, detail
Andō Hiroshige (Japanese, 1797–1858); Edo period
Colored woodblock print; 8⁵⁄₁₆ x 11³⁄₁₆ in.
Bequest of Mrs. H. O. Havemeyer, 1929, H. O. Havemeyer Collec-
  tion, Japanese print 1899

PAGE 24. *Chrysanthemums*, detail
Claude Monet (French, 1840–1926); dated 1882
Oil on canvas; 39½ x 32¼ in.
Bequest of Mrs. H. O. Havemeyer, 1929, H. O. Havemeyer Collec-
  tion, 29.100.106

PAGE 25. *Woman's Ceremonial Robe*, detail
Artist unknown (Chinese, late 19th century); Ch'ing dynasty
Silk-warp twill embroidered in colored silks, couched with silk
  threads wrapped in gold; length 55 in.
Bequest of Duchesse de Richelieu, in memory of Captain Frederick
  May Wise, U.S.N., 1972, 1973.28.4

PAGES 26–27. *A Woman with Chrysanthemums*, detail
Edgar Degas (French, 1834–1917); dated 1858 and 1865
Oil on canvas; 29 x 36½ in.
Bequest of Mrs. H. O. Havemeyer, 1929, H. O. Havemeyer Collec-
  tion, 29.100.128

PAGES 28–29. *Iris*, detail
Katsushika Hokusai (Japanese, 1760–1849); Tokugawa period
Colored woodblock print; 9³/₄ x 14³/₁₆ in.
Frederick C. Hewitt Fund, 1911, Japanese print 747

PAGE 30. *Iris and Bridge*, detail
Ogata Kōrin (Japanese, 1658–1716); Edo period
Six-panel screen; ink, colors, and gold leaf on paper; 70½ x 146¼ in.
Purchase, Louisa Eldridge McBurney Gift, 1953, 53.7.2

PAGE 31. *Irises and Wild Roses*
John LaFarge (American, 1835–1910); 1887
Watercolor on paper; 12⁵/₈ x 10¹/₈ in.
Gift of Priscilla A. B. Henderson, in memory of her grandfather,
  Russell S. Sturgis, a founder of the Museum, 1950, 50.113.3

PAGES 32–33. *Irises*
Vincent van Gogh (Dutch, 1853–1890); 1890
Oil on canvas; 29 x 36¼ in.
Gift of Adele R. Levy, 1958, 58.187

PAGE 34. *Sunflowers*
Vincent van Gogh (Dutch, 1853–1890); 1887
Oil on canvas; 17 x 24 in.
Rogers Fund, 1949, 49.41

PAGE 35. *Sunflowers*
Claude Monet (French, 1840–1926); dated 1881
Oil on canvas; 39³/₄ x 32 in.
Bequest of Mrs. H. O. Havemeyer, 1929, H. O. Havemeyer Collec-
  tion, 29.100.107

PAGE 36. *Hybrid Amaryllis (Hippeastrum Regina-vittata)*
William Say (British, 1768–1834) after B. Cotton (British, 19th
  century)
From *Transactions of the Horticultural Society of London*, 1824
Hand-colored engraving; 16³/₈ x 11⁵/₈ in.
Harris Brisbane Dick Fund, 1924, 24.66.367(5)

PAGE 37. *Amaryllis*
Mary Frank (American, 1933–); 1977
Color monotype in two parts; each part 17³/₄ x 23³/₄ in.
Steward S. MacDermott Fund, 1977, 1977.550 (a&b)

PAGES 38–39. *Nō Robe for a Female Role*, whole and detail
Artist unknown (Japanese, late 17th or early 18th century)
Silk-warp twill with silk floss and flat gold yarns *(kara-ori);* length
  53 in.
Purchase, Joseph Pulitzer Bequest, 1932, 32.30.7

PAGES 40–41. *Tree Peonies*, whole and detail
Yun Shou-p'ing (Chinese, 1633–1690); Ch'ing dynasty
Hanging scroll, ink and colors on silk; 69½ x 35¹/₈ in.
Gift of Mr. and Mrs. Earl Morse, 1972, 1972.16

PAGES 42–43, 44. *Tughra*, details
Artist unknown (Turkish, 16th century)
Calligraphic emblem from an imperial edict of Sulaymān the
  Magnificent
Ink, colors, and gold on paper; 20½ x 23¼ in.
Rogers Fund, 1938, 38.149.2

PAGE 45. *Pink*
"Moreljon," from a sketchbook of flowers
Artist unknown (Netherlandish, 17th century)
Watercolor; height 9¼ in.
Anonymous Gift, 1946, 46.8.11(11)

PAGE 46. *Lady with a Pink*
Attributed to Hans Memling (Flemish,
active about 1465–died 1494)
Tempera and oil on wood; 17 x 7¼ in.
The Jules Bache Collection, 1949, 49.7.23

PAGE 47. *Lady with a Pink*
Rembrandt van Rijn (Dutch, 1606–1669)
Oil on canvas; 36¼ x 29³/₈ in.
Bequest of Benjamin Altman, 1913, 14.40.622

PAGES 48–49. *Madonna and Child with Angels*,
whole and detail
Cosimo Rosselli (Italian, Florentine, 1439–1507)
Tempera on wood; 33½ x 23 in.
Bequest of Michael Friedsam, 1931, The Michael
Friedsam Collection, 32.100.84

PAGE 50. *The Toilet of Venus*
François Boucher (French, 1703–1770); 1751
Oil on canvas; 42⁵/₈ x 33½ in.
Bequest of William K. Vanderbilt, 1920, 20.155.9

PAGE 51. *The Love Letter*
Jean Honoré Fragonard (French, 1732–1806)
Oil on canvas; 32³/₄ x 26³/₈ in.
The Jules Bache Collection, 1949, 49.7.49

PAGES 52–53. *The Hunt of the Unicorn*, details
Artists unknown (Franco-Flemish, 16th century)
Tapestry, wool and silk, silver-gilt threads; 68½ x 25½ in.
Gift of John D. Rockefeller, Jr., 1938, 38.51.1

PAGES 54–55. *Rubens and His Wife, Hélène Fourment, with Their
  Child*, whole and detail
Peter Paul Rubens (Flemish, 1577–1640)
Oil on wood; 80³/₈ x 62⁵/₈ in.
Gift of Mr. and Mrs. Charles Wrightsman, 1981, 1981.238

PAGES 56–57. *Pink Roses with Wasps*, detail
Artist unknown (Chinese, Ch'ing dynasty, 1644–1911)
Handscroll, colors on silk; 9¹⁵/₁₆ x 79⁵/₈ in.
Fletcher Fund, 1947, 47.18.5

PAGE 58. *Path in the Ile Saint-Martin, Vétheuil*, detail
Claude Monet (French, 1840–1926); 1880
Oil on canvas; 31½ x 23³/₄ in.
Bequest of Julia W. Emmons, 1956, 56.135.1

PAGE 59. *Still Life with Poppy, Insects, and Reptiles*
Otto Marseus van Schrieck (Dutch, 1619–1678)
Oil on canvas; 26⁷/₈ x 20³/₄ in.
Rogers Fund, 1953, 53.155

PAGES 60-61. *Poppies*, whole and detail
School of Sōtatsu, style of Kitagawa Sosetsu (Japanese, mid-17th century); Edo period
Colors on gold paper; 34½ x 14⅝ in.
Bequest of Mrs. H. O. Havemeyer, 1929, H. O. Havemeyer Collection, 29.100.524

PAGE 62. *Bridge over a Pool of Water Lilies*, detail
Claude Monet (French, 1840–1926); 1899
Oil on canvas; 36½ x 29 in.
Bequest of Mrs. H. O. Havemeyer, 1929, H. O. Havemeyer Collection, 29.100.113

PAGE 63. *Waterlilies*
E. A. Séguy (French, active 1920s)
From *Les Fleurs et leurs applications décoratives*
Lithograph; 19¾ x 14½ in.
Purchase, Leon Lowenstein Foundation, Inc., Gift, 1976, 1976.581

PAGE 64. *Study of Tulips*
Jacob Marrel (Dutch, 1614–1681); 1636
Watercolor on vellum; 13⁹⁄₁₆ x 17¹⁵⁄₁₆ in.
Rogers Fund, 1968, 68.66

PAGE 65. *Bouquet of Flowers in a Crystal Vase*
Nicolaes van Veerendael (Flemish, 1640–1691); 1662
Oil on canvas; 20⅛ x 16½ in.
Bequest of Stephen Whitney Phoenix, 1881, 81.1.652

PAGE 66. *Hummingbird and Passionflowers*
Martin Johnson Heade (American, 1817–1904)
Oil on canvas; 20 x 12 in.
Gift of Albert Weatherby, 1946, 46.17

PAGE 67. *Orchids*
Ma Lin (Chinese, active about 1250); Southern Sung dynasty
Leaf from an album; ink and colors on silk; 10⅜ x 8¹³⁄₁₆ in.
Gift of The Dillon Fund, 1973, 1973.120.10

PAGES 68–69. *Fraktur Motifs*
Johan Henrich Otto (American, late 18th century)
Pen and watercolor on paper; 13⅛ x 16½ in.
Gift of Edgar William and Bernice Chrysler Garbisch, 1966, 66.242.1

PAGE 70. *Compton*, detail
William Morris (British, 1834–1896); 1896
Wallpaper; 22 inches wide
Purchase, Edward C. Moore, Jr. Gift, 1923, 23.163.4(e)

PAGE 71. *Sample for an Embroidered Waistcoat*, detail
Artist unknown (French, early 19th century)
Silk on silk; 13¼ x 11⅛ in.
Gift of United Piece Dye Works, 1936, 36.90.15

PAGES 72–73. *Hanging*, whole and detail
Artist unknown (Iranian, 19th century)
Wool embroidered in silk; 75 x 50 in.
Rogers Fund, 1910, 10.33.1

PAGES 74–75. *Vase*, whole and detail
Artist unknown (Chinese, late 17th–early 18th century); Ch'ing dynasty
Enamels painted on the biscuit; height 29¼ in.
Bequest of Benjamin Altman, 1913, 14.40.401

PAGE 76. *Girl with a Lantern on a Balcony at Night*
Suzuki Harunobu (Japanese, 1725–1770); Edo period
Colored woodblock print; 12¾ x 8¼ in.
Fletcher Fund, 1929, Japanese print 1506

PAGE 77. *Lacquer Box*, detail
Artist unknown (Japanese, 17th century); Edo period
Leather, lacquer, and mother-of-pearl lid; 11 x 14¾ in.
Fletcher Fund, 1925, 25.215.57

PAGE 78. *Flowering Tree, Possibly Quince*
Artist unknown (Indian, 17th century); Mughal period
Leaf from an album; ink, colors, and gold on paper; 10³⁄₁₆ x 7 in.
Bequest of Cora Timken Burnett, 1956, Cora Timken Burnett Collection of Persian Miniatures and Other Persian Art Objects, 1956, 57.51.34

PAGE 79. *Wedding Hanging*, detail
Artist unknown (Chinese, early 18th century); Ch'ing dynasty
Satin embroidered in colored silks, couched with wrapped gold; 83 x 37 in.
Gift of Albert Gallatin Lanier, 1977, 1977.321.2

PAGE 80. *Man and Woman Arranging Flowers*
Kitagawa Utamaro (Japanese, 1753–1806); Edo period
A scene from act 4 of the drama *Chūsingura: Loyal Retainers of the 47 Ronin*
Colored woodblock print; 15⅛ x 10⅛ in.
Gift of Mrs. J. Watson Webb, 1930, H. O. Havemeyer Collection, Japanese print 2393

PAGE 81. *Mount Fuji and Flowers*
David Hockney (British, 1937–)
Acrylic on canvas; 60 x 48 in.
Purchase, Mrs. Arthur Hays Sulzberger
Gift in memory of Arthur Hays Sulzberger, 1972, 1972.128

PAGE 82. *Bouquet of Flowers*
Odilon Redon (French, 1840–1916)
Pastel on paper; 31⅝ x 25¼ in.
Gift of Mrs. George B. Post, 1956, 56.50

PAGE 83. *A Vase with Flowers*
Jacob Vosmaer (Dutch, 1584–1641); 1615
Oil on wood; 33½ x 24⅝ in.
Purchase, 1871, 71.5

PAGE 84. *Basket of Flowers*
Marie-Claude-Sophie Xhrouet (French, active 1772–1778); 1773
Sèvres plaque set in an upright secretary by Martin Carlin
Soft-paste porcelain; 12½ x 9⅝ in.
Gift of Samuel H. Kress Foundation, 1958, 58.75.44

PAGE 85. *Vase of Flowers*
Anne Vallayer-Coster (French, 1744–1818); 1780
Oil on canvas; 19¾ x 15 in.
Gift of J. Pierpont Morgan, 1906, 07.225.504

PAGE 86. *Pansies on a Table*
Henri Matisse (French, 1869–1954)
Oil on paper; 19¼ x 17¾ in.
Bequest of Joan Whitney Payson, 1975, 1976.201.22

PAGE 87. *Mauve Primulas on a Table*
Sir William Nicholson (British, 1872–1949)
Oil on wood; 23¾ x 16¾ in.
Bequest of Mary Cushing Fosburgh, 1978, 1979.135.15

PAGES 88–89. *Still Life with Pansies*
Ignace Henri Jean Théodore Fantin-Latour (French, 1836–1904);
  1874
Oil on canvas; 18½ x 22¼ in.
The Mr. and Mrs. Henry Ittleson, Jr. Purchase Fund, 1966, 66.194

PAGE 90. *Still Life: Apples and a Pot of Primroses*
Paul Cézanne (French, 1839–1906)
Oil on canvas; 28¾ x 36⅜ in.
Bequest of Sam A. Lewisohn, 1951, 51.112.2

PAGE 91. *Still Life with Flowers and Fruit*
Ignace Henri Jean Théodore Fantin-Latour (French, 1836–1904);
  1866
Oil on canvas; 28¾ x 23⅝ in.
Purchase, Mr. and Mrs. Richard J. Bernhard Gift, by exchange, 1980,
  1980.3

PAGES 92–93. *Armoire à deux corps*, whole and detail
Artist unknown (French, Burgundian?, late 16th century)
Walnut, carved, gilded, and painted; 97 x 61½ x 25 in.
Rogers Fund, 1925, 25.181

PAGES 94–95. *Fall-front Secretary*, whole and detail
Part of a bedroom suite by Herter Brothers
  (American, working 1865/66–1905/6); 1882
Cherry, ebonized, marquetry; 54 x 34⅛ x 19 in.
Gift of Paul Martini, 1969, 69.146.3

PAGE 96. *Four Seasons: Spring*, detail
Embroidered hanging attributed to the Convent of Saint-Joseph de la
  Providence (French, late 17th century)
Wool, silk, and metal threads on canvas; 164 x 108 in.
Rogers Fund, 1946, 46.43.1

PAGE 97. *Spring*
Mary Wright (American, 18th century); 1754
Canvas embroidered in colored wools; 7⅝ x 7⅝ in.
Rogers Fund, 1946, 46.155

PAGES 98–99. *Baltimore Album Quilt*, whole and detail
Attributed to Mary Evans (American, 19th century); 1845–50
Cotton, printed and unprinted, appliquéd in silk and velvet;
  104¾ x 103½ in.
Sansbury-Mills Fund, 1974, 1974.24

PAGES 100–101. *Still Life: A Basket of Flowers*
Jan Brueghel the Younger (Flemish, 1601–1678)
Oil on wood; 18½ x 26⅞ in.
Bequest of Miss Adelaide Milton de Groot, 1967, 67.187.58

PAGES 102–103. *Basket of Flowers*
Eugène Delacroix (French, 1798–1863); 1848
Oil on canvas; 42¼ x 56 in.
Bequest of Miss Adelaide Milton de Groot, 1967, 67.187.60

PAGES 104–105. *Yellow Basket of Flowers*
Artist unknown (American, second quarter 19th century)
Watercolor on paper; 15¾ x 19⅝ in.
Gift of Edgar William and Bernice Chrysler Garbisch, 1966,
  66.242.4

PAGES 106–107. *Landscape, Fruit and Flowers*
Fanny F. Palmer (American, 19th century) for Currier & Ives; 1862
Hand-colored lithograph; 19⅞ x 27½ in.
Bequest of Adele S. Colgate, 1962, 63.550.262

PAGES 108–111. Details from *A Day in a Child's Life*
Hand-colored wood engravings after drawings by Kate Greenaway
  (British, 1846–1901); 1881
Volume; 9⅝ x 8¼ in.
Jacob S. Rogers Fund, 1921, 21.36.91

PAGE 112. *Watch*
Casemaker: L. C.; movement by Grayhurst, Harvey and Company
  (British, working 1805–1830); 1819/20
Case of *basse taille* enamel on gold with pearls; diam. 2⅜ in.
Bequest of Laura Frances Hearn, 1917, 17.101.70

BACK ENDPAPER. *Iris and Bridge*, detail
Ogata Kōrin (Japanese, 1658–1716); Edo period
Six-panel screen; ink, colors, and gold leaf on paper; 70½ x 146¼ in.
Purchase, Louisa Eldridge McBurney Gift, 1953, 53.7.2

Manufactured by Grayhurst, Harvey and Company of London for the China market in the early nineteenth century, the watchcase is framed by rows of pearls. The surface, initialed L. C., was created by an enamel technique knows as *basse taille*. The red enamel fused to gold engraved in relief is prettily painted with a bouquet of blossoms including the rose and peony—two flowers of singular symbolic and historic import to the Chinese.

Flowers, so beautiful yet so short-lived, often symbolize the intense pleasures and poignant briefness of human life and love. Poets, both major and minor, have often lamented that our joys are as fleeting as the extravagant blossoms of spring and summer. The poet Pierre de Ronsard (1524–1585) speaks for many when he observes: "All that is beautiful is transient too/Lilies and roses have brief days and few."

This watch is a witty reversal of this theme—it marks the passage of time, but the flowers on its case will never fade.